LOUISIANA'S CAPITOLS
THE POWER AND THE BEAUTY

The Louisiana State Capitol building and the Old State Capitol lie along the banks of the Mississippi River about a mile apart. Between them is downtown Baton Rouge. In the distance are petrochemical plants that have propelled the area's economy. (Opposite page) The Huey Long statue over his grave in front of the State Capitol

LOUISIANA'S
THE POWER AND THE BEAUTY
CAPITOLS

Photographs by Philip Gould

Text by Lawrence N. Powell

GALERIE PRESS

LAFAYETTE, LOUISIANA

Library of Congress # 94-073040

ISBN# 0917-541-03-0

Book design: John Langston

Production: Chip Blackshear

Linotronics: Baton Rouge Printing Co.

Editorial Assistance: Sandy Hebert LaBry

Printing: Dai Nippon Printing Co. Ltd.

Manufactured in Hong Kong

First Printing 1995

GALERIE PRESS

Mailing Address: P.O. Box 4608
                      Lafayette, LA 70502

Shipping Address: Route 3, Box 252
                      Arnaudville, LA 70512

Telephone: (318) 662-5295
Telefax: (318) 662-3259

Front Cover: Interior light illuminates the stained glass window of the Old State Capitol's House chamber.

Back Cover: Representative Jimmy Dimos visits with House colleagues prior to a session in the new State Capitol.

DEDICATION

This book is dedicated to the memory of my father Arthur J. Gould,
a political enthusiast and life-long Republican, as well as to my aunt Mary Dau,
a career diplomat with the Danish Ministry of Foreign Affairs and authority
on Soviet relations. Over the years they both instilled in me an
appreciation of politics as well as diplomacy and history.

This book is made possible in part by a grant from
The Louisiana Endowment for the Humanities

CONTENTS

In 1827, Louisiana's Spanish-era state house burned leaving the government homeless. State officials then moved into the Ursuline Convent in New Orleans where they conducted business in 1828, 1829, and 1831. In 1830, the state's capitol moved to Donaldsonville. The legislature met there for only one year before returning to New Orleans. This frieze (opposite page) on the House of Representatives' door in today's Capitol is one of the few visual records of the Donaldsonville capitol. Sculptors crafted the frieze according to details in the original 1825 construction contract.

CAPITOL WANDERINGS

Standing within hailing distance of each other above the Baton Rouge levee, Louisiana's two state capitols evoke a sense of permanence. First, there was the Gothic castle in which the dominion's pre-Huey history seemingly unfolded with genteel decorum. Then came the Jazz Age and a soaring Art Deco skyscraper sheathed in Alabama limestone heralding a new Kingfish of the realm. The leap from castle to skyscraper admittedly marks a sharp break in state history, like the Mississippi jumping its banks. But the buildings themselves symbolize reassuring stability. If Louisiana politics have been marred by scandal, assassination, and revolution, at least the seat of government seems to have stayed put.

But even that is not true. For the first seventy years of statehood, Louisiana's capital remained unsettled. Originally it was in New Orleans. Then it moved to the sugar growing center of Donaldsonville. Then it returned to New Orleans. Next came Baton Rouge. During the Civil War Opelousas and Shreve-

port won the honor of feeding Confederate state officials. After the Crescent City fell to the Yankees, New Orleans' turn came up again. Altogether, between 1812 and 1882, the capital shifted eleven times among six different cities. Baton Rouge did not become the definitive location until the 19th century's waning decades.

The upheavals of War and Reconstruction had a lot to do with the capital's early wander-

ings. But the real reason for the instability was rural Louisiana's resolve to restrict New Orleans' political power.

The tension between city and country is as old as the state itself. Justly famous for its complex politics, Louisiana is a melange of distinct cultures that have not co-existed well. The Anglo-Baptist North feared—and still does—the fun-loving Franco-Catholic South. Big sugar and cotton planters from the delta scorned populists from the hills and piney woods. Deep cleavages of race and class— even modern ethnicity, due to the state's unsouthern experience with immigration— have also shaped the Louisiana political landscape. But overlaying and antedating them all has been the rural-urban split, doubtless because New Orleans was the South's largest metropolis until well into the 20th century. Today that fault line symbolizes sharp racial divisions. But in the 19th century, when debates raged over where to locate the capital, the city-country antagonism was especially acute.

Whether French or English-speaking, the country parishes remained restless while New Orleans was the seat of government. The anxiety mounted once trade from the Mississippi Valley transformed the city into a New World colossus of commerce and pleasure. Rural politicians distrusted New Orleans' concentrated power. They disliked its prying press corps. They dreaded its hooliganism. Most of all, they were ambivalent about its libidinal distractions.

In 1829, the legislature committed self-denial by voting to move the capital fifty miles upriver to Donaldsonville. The original state house, located on the corner of Toulouse and Decatur in the French Quarter, had burned down two years earlier. Constructed in 1761, the year before France transferred Louisiana to Spain, the Government House, as it was known, was a hip-roofed, two-story Creole structure girdled by arcaded galleries. A lot of interesting history had transpired within its walls: the sentencing to death of LaFranière and his fellow conspirators, for instance, or the consultation between General James Wilkinson and Governor William C. C. Claiborne to checkmate Aaron Burr's alleged conspiracy to recapture the Mississippi Valley for Spain. But by the time the building caught on fire, the structure was fairly dilapidated, and city fire fighters were too inebriated to contain the blaze. The legislature, which was still in session, immediately reconvened in the

Orleans Theater—remembered today for its quadroon balls. A few days later it moved into the top floor of the Ursuline Convent, which was then occupied by New Orleans' only high school. The arrangement was makeshift at best, which is doubtless why lawmakers voted to move to Donaldsonville, appropriating $30,000 to construct a new state house.[1]

The 1830 legislature convened in the sugar growing hamlet at the head waters of Bayou LaFourche, but the exile was short-lived. The winter that year was unusually cold and rainy. Donaldsonville's cuisine was as dreary as the weather. Entertainment outlets were nil. Committee quorums became impossible when members began catching New Orleans-bound steamboats for early-bird weekends. In 1831 the legislature repented its decision and hurried back to the city. The following year the state purchased the old Charity Hospital to house the departments of government.

The capital was moved again by the Constitutional Convention of 1845. The 1845 Constitution was a watershed in state political history, marking the ascendancy of Americans over Creoles and ushering in long overdue democratic reforms. The upstate Jacksonians who dominated the convention seized the moment to straitjacket the city. Explosive growth had propelled New Orleans overnight into the nation's fourth largest metropolis. Rural forces feared that "the country will truly be swallowed up by the overshadowing influence and power of the city . . . ."[2] They

attacked New Orleans' power on two fronts: by restricting the number of seats the city could control in future legislatures, and by removing the capital from the city. In order to hold onto as many seats as possible, the Orleans delegation acquiesced in the pressure to relocate the capital.

One reason city members gave in so easily was their understanding of lawmaker foibles. "Place the capitol within sixty miles of New Orleans," a city delegate taunted the convention, "and you will find it impossible to keep the members away from the city; some will come to attend to their business; some for the purpose of enjoying the winter amusements of the city; and the consequence will be that your public buildings will be deserted."[3] The rural majority had an answer to that one. The removal provision directed that the capital be situated "not less than sixty miles from the city of New Orleans, by the nearest traveling route," and discouraged legislative backtracking by requiring four-fifths approval for future relocation. City members protested that the super majority requirement stifled popular will. Country delegates had a response to that one, too. "It is not the popular will they desire to restrict, but the legislative will," one rural member said.[4]

The removal amendment failed to specify where the capital would go. But it was a foregone conclusion that Baton Rouge would win the competition. The town lay beyond the sixty mile pleasure limit, yet was close enough to the city for weekend jaunts. Moreover, its boosters and town lot speculators had purchased the Thomas Gibbes Morgan estate near the levee, offering it free as a capitol site. The Morgan property was the first high land visible to steamboats ascending the river.[5]

There was a last minute snag. According to the 1845 Constitution, the next legislature had exactly one month to choose a new state capital. Donaldsonville and Baton Rouge were the chief contestants, but New Orleans was still in the hunt. One city lawmaker proposed a constitutional amendment designating New Orleans the permanent seat of government and found upstate support. Declared Senator Taylor from Natchitoches: "...one of the principal inducements to many of the members of the Legislature to become candidates for their seats was the pleasures of city life for two or three months." The 1846 legislature ultimately awarded Baton Rouge the site for fear too much wrangling might cause the legislature to miss the thirty-day deadline. The governor signed the legislation on March 9, 1846, the day the clock ran out.[6]

During the Civil War, the capital returned to New Orleans for a spell. In 1864, while the Confederate state officials were retreating toward Shreveport, New Orleans Unionists wrote a new constitution restoring the seat of government to the Crescent City. Three years later, after black enfranchisement gave Louisiana Republicans a voting majority, the reconstructionists also made New Orleans the capital. Like their predecessors, however, they never did get around to building a real capitol in the city. They made do with hand-me-downs. The Republican legislature and governor initially took up residence in the old Mechanics Institute near Rampart and Canal Streets. During one particularly stormy session, a group of legislative bolters even set up shop in a Royal Street saloon. From 1874 to 1877, the state operated out of the St. Louis Hotel in the French Quarter, at the spot now occupied by the Omni Royal Orleans.

In 1879, the Redeemers who forcibly overthrew Reconstruction met in New Orleans to draft another constitution (the third in

fifteen years). They rehashed old debates concerning New Orleans' vices and virtues—mainly vices. The city's sensate temptations were the focus of attention. Explained an East Carroll cotton planter: "The attractions of Baton Rouge were not so fascinating as to lead members astray from their duty. Committees could always get quorums to do their work when the capitol was at Baton Rouge, which was the reverse here." The convention voted, 84-24, to return the seat of government to Baton Rouge. "Nearly all the country members voted in the affirmative," reported the *Daily Picayune*, "while the city almost unanimously voted in the negative."[7] The 1882 homecoming proved permanent.

If the capital had left New Orleans for good, that hardly meant New Orleans had left the capitol. New Orleanians built and restored Baton Rouge's Gothic castle. They designed Huey's skyscraper, deciding which history lessons it would teach in stone. The structures have a Crescent City ambiance. It is as though the ghosts of legislators past brought the party with them.

Mounted on the gate in front of the Old State Capitol is an ax bundled with bamboo rods. Known as a "fasces", this ancient Roman symbol implied power and authority. Mussolini adopted it as the namesake of his Fascist Party in the 1920s. New door handles (opposite page) were created for the Old State Capitol's 1994 restoration.

LOUISIANA GOTHIC

It is a minor mystery why the first capitol built in Baton Rouge wasn't a Greek Revival temple. Everywhere else in antebellum America champions of the common man were making "Greek Revival their emblem."[1] After the national capitol set the fashion, legislatures insisted on erecting dome-portico-matching wing capitols. Louisiana (and, to a lesser extent, Georgia) is the great exception. Here a Gothic Revival capitol was built on a bluff overlooking the Father of Waters. If monumental architecture reflects the dominant values of the time, it is worth asking what cultural forces found expression in the old state capitol. The monarchism of Louisiana's colonial past? The cocksuredness of her plantation laborlords? The state's strong Catholic heritage? Part of the answer is a New Orleans sense of fun.

Louisiana could easily have afforded to lavish money on its new capitol. The state in 1850 was fabulously wealthy. The competition among town boosters, however, kept the initial appropriation at only $100,000. (The final price tag would ultimately triple.) The low figure ruled out constructing a stone and marble neo-classical temple.

The legislature designated three commissioners to take responsibility for siting and building the new capitol. The leader was wealthy sugar planter Maunsel White, a self-made Ulster Irishman famous for his signature hot sauce. (Another hot sauce impresario, Daniel Avery, founder of Avery Island, also served on the commission.) State Senator White, who shared the southern gentry's fondness for architecture, looked to New Orleans for guidance. The city's dominance in this field was largely due to three architects—James Dakin, his younger brother Charles, and James Gallier—all products of the founding firm of American architecture, the New York-based Town and Davis.[2]

The Dakin brothers and Gallier, who came to New Orleans in the mid-1830s, built their reputation on Greek Revival architecture. Several years earlier James Dakin sought to build a Greek Revival capitol in New Orleans. But five days after the legislature had authorized bidding on the Baton Rouge contract, the New Orleans architect had readied a different set of plans. Neo-classical models had become stale and hackneyed, he wrote. In place of Greek Revival, he recommended "the Castellated Gothic style. . . ."[3] Dakin had already built several Gothic churches, including St. Patrick's Cathedral in New

Orleans. But the proposed Louisiana capitol, with its battlements and turrets, was a new departure even for him. More than any of his previous neo-Gothic conceptions, Dakin's design seemed to march straight out of the Middle Ages. The commission nonetheless chose his proposal.

Dakin stressed financial considerations in his pitch to the commission: "A building could be erected according to the design for $100,000 using brick and cement for the walls and cast iron for the window frames and ornamental details."[4] As it finally happened, Dakin covered most of the building's brick exterior with stucco, which he scored to imitate stone blocks.[4] And he slashed costs even further by making liberal use of cast iron, a new structural material.

The genius of Dakin's Gothic Revival design inhered in its responsiveness to popular trends. Antebellum Americans were enraptured with Sir Walter Scott's romantic novels and their vivid descriptions of medieval landscapes. They showed their enthusiasm by Gothicizing everything from churches to barns and kennels. The Crescent City's infatuation with Scott gushed onto the local stage, where adaptations of his stories played to packed houses, and into Mardi Gras. When Uptown Protestants incorporated Creole carnival into their status hierarchy, organizing it around socially exclusive krewes and mock-chivalric tableaux, they drew heavily on Sir Walter.[5]

Dakin's Norman castle (and church, too, since the building follows a cruciform outline)

was obviously inspired by Scott. But the elliptical glass dome he surmounted slightly off-center also betrays local influences. State capitols usually have domes, to inspire civic reverence. However, Dakin's translucent ellipse was installed for ballroom effect. Shortly after the capitol opened, Baton Rougeans began using the rotunda for dances and other festive occasions. In fact, by 1858, the building had become, in the words of Dakin's biographer, Arthur Scully, "a virtual center of social activity in the primitive capital of Louisiana when the legislature was not in session."[6]

In other commonwealths the idea of marrying Xanadu to Westminister Abbey is hard to take seriously. But 19th century Louisianians—or at least New Orleanians—never built public buildings strictly for civic ceremony. They expected their public places to double as social arenas. Dakin had lived long enough in New Orleans to understand its rhythms. That is probably why he decided to graft a pleasure dome onto a legislative cathedral.

Dakin met difficulty translating his conception into bricks and mortar. Powerful legislators attacked his fee. One senator sneered at Dakin's professional credentials as an architect. "There was no necessity for employing this man of theory," he told the 1847 legislature. "Set aside the architect for a practical builder." The critics slashed Dakin's fee by 40 percent.[7]

The capitol project was such a drain on his resources that Dakin threatened to quit. His patron Maunsel White, however, was adamant about holding him to the contract. "You are aware of the general dislike there is throughout the State to the present location," White explained to the younger man, "and there are hundreds who would lay hold on any pretext to defeat the erection of the building even at the risk of destroying your, mine or anyone else's character, no matter could they attain their ends." Dakin stayed on the job.

There was trouble with some of the building material as well. A perennial problem was the quality of the bricks—all 4,039,786 of them. In Louisiana's hot, soggy climate it was essential that they be "good hard burnt bricks," to use White's words, but the vendor, McHatton, Pratt, and Company, kept sending half-baked ones. The company leased convicts from the state to fabricate its bricks, with poor results.

One sweltering August day in 1848, Dakin climbed onto the scaffolding and began tossing soft bricks over the wall. By his own admission, he discarded a lot of them. Witnesses said he even yanked defective bricks from freshly mortared walls. When Pratt, the on-site partner, approached him angrily, Dakin threw a punch. The two men exchanged blows before being separated. Covered with blood, Pratt returned a short while later with a pistol; at some point during the fracas Dakin drew his sword. Neither man was injured. The next day the mayor had both men arrested and fined.[8]

In 1848, the legislature authorized an additional $100,000 for embellishments—one of the few bright spots for Dakin. The extra money made it possible to furnish the interior and adorn grounds with botanical and zoological gardens. In 1852, the legislature appropriated over $21,000 for the cast iron fence that surrounds the capitol.[9]

Dakin had to have been disappointed with the critical reception accorded his building. During the 1852 legislative session, the New Orleans *Daily Delta* savaged the capitol as an "unsightly mass. . . only fit for an insane asylum." A day earlier the New Orleans *Daily Crescent* declared: "The architect has been given the license to construct a bauble as useless and unnecessary in architecture as the writing-master's flourish. . . The building should have been of the Grecian order, instead of the anomalous Gothic style adopted by the commissioners."[10]

Dakin died three months later, at age 46, from "a long and painful illness."[11]

It remained for another New Orleans architect to put the finishing touch on Dakin's neo-Gothic creation. The building had been all but destroyed by a fire accidentally started in 1862, by Union soldiers cooking breakfast in the basement. Flames completely gutted the structure, destroying the state library and all the furnishings. Over the next two decades the capitol stood abandoned. Livestock trampled expensive shrubbery. Local residents carted off everything that was not bolted down, and a few iron railings that were. Seen through the moonlight from afar, the capitol resembled one of those medieval ruins over which English romantic poets used to swoon. In 1866, a *Harper's Weekly* reporter wrote from his steamer, as the capitol hove into view: "our young country . . . has no other ruin so fine." But up close the scene was squalor.[12]

In 1879, after voting to relocate the capital to Baton Rouge, lawmakers appropriated funds to restore Dakin's castle. The following year former New Orleans mayor and then governor Louis Wiltz awarded William A. Freret, who had built several of the city's McDonogh schools, the state contract for doing the renovations. He completed the project in 1882.[13]

Fortunately, the exterior walls were structurally sound. Construction estimates came in at roughly $200,000—a very cheap price tag, according to a national architectural magazine.[14] Freret moved the capitol's main entrance from the river front to the northern facade, creating a recessed vestibule leading directly into the rotunda. He added a fourth floor in the central part of the structure, to make room for an expanded state bureaucracy. And he built a much larger glass dome in the rotunda, capping it with a hot house-like "lantern" to solve the leaking problem that had plagued Dakin's original ellipse. The "lantern" rose another two stories above the roof. For good measure Freret candied up the exterior with a lot of Gothicized frosting: six cast iron cylindrical turrets, twelve miniature bartizan towers on the corners, and so on.

The most famous criticism of Louisiana's "little sham castle" came from Mark Twain. But his memorable eruption was triggered by the Freret restoration, not the Dakin original. "It is pathetic enough," Twain wrote in his *Life on the Mississippi*, "that a whitewashed castle, with turrets and things—materials all ungenuine within and without—should ever have been built in this otherwise honorable place; but it is much more pathetic to see this architectural falsehood undergoing restoration and perpetualization in our day, when it would have been so easy to let dynamite finish what a charitable fire began, and then devote this restoration money to the building of something genuine."[15]

Traveling by steamboat to New Orleans, Twain never went inside the old capitol, so he overlooked the sole modification that was authentic: the glass dome. Exfoliating from a cast iron column shooting from a coiled staircase connecting the first two floors, Freret's vaulted fan infused technicolor whimsy into the once dim rotunda. The New Orleans architect had set out to solve a lighting problem, but he created an enchanted atmosphere. Mad Hatter balls and March Hare fantasies filled the air. Freret also tessellated the marble floors into a twisted checkerboard, but that architectural detail only enhanced the Alice-in-Wonderland effect.[16]

Critics have praised Freret's rotunda as "an uninhibited Victorian ode to the iron age." They have drawn analogies to the

Crystal Palace in London.[17] With one vertical thrust he connected Gothic Revival with High Victorianism. But Louisiana influences closer to home furnished inspiration as well. New Orleans merriment driped from the arched tracery of the rotunda's bayed gallery.

Freret's glassed rotunda survived his exterior modifications to Dakin's castle. The cast-iron turrets were removed in 1907. Locals belittled the bartizan towers as so many "buzzard roosts." They came down in 1937.[18] The refurbished castle remained the home of state government until 1932, when the legislature and bureaucracy were transferred to Huey Long's skyscraper. The building was considered an embarrassment, defying what an American capitol was supposed to look like. It never could escape Twain's derision.

A half century elapsed before the state got around to restoring the historic structure. It reopened as Louisiana's Center for Political and Governmental History on May 1, 1994.

Begun in 1982, the on-again, off-again renovation took twelve years to complete— four times longer than the original construction. Of itself the drawn out process should not occasion surprise. Historic restoration is painstaking work. It involves a huge amount of sleuthing, a lot of sifting, tagging, and analysis. The old capitol reconstruction was also plagued by hard fiscal realities and politics, especially the ancient antagonism between New Orleans and Baton Rouge.

The project architect for the restoration was New Orleans-born and Tulane-educated Eean McNaughton, a Scots perfectionist with a wry sense of humor. "I have never done replicative architecture and don't ever intend to," he says. In the mid-seventies he served as project architect for the Old Mint restoration in the French Quarter. McNaughton received the Old Capitol after preservationists protested political interference in the selection process.[19]

McNaughton is a strong believer in internationally-recognized standards of restorative architecture. "There was a very pivotal conference held in Venice, Italy, in the early 'sixties that set principles for historic restoration," he said. The basic tenet is that an artifact should be enjoyed as an artifact. McNaughton explained: "The restorative architect shouldn't intervene in the original design, even if it contains features we no longer value or admire. And if he is forced to make modifications they should be obvious." Modern safety codes put those standards to the test. McNaughton had to install interior fire stairs. To avoid disrupting the outside window pattern, he decided to pull the stair back from the wall. "This way you don't have the stair running right across the face of the window," he said. "The stair has its freedom, and it is obvious that it is a new piece."

If restoration architecture is essentially the art of recovery, it was clear from the outset that McNaughton would have to begin from two different historical baselines. For the exterior restoration he looked to Dakin's original 1847 conception—ignoring the fourth floor and roof "lantern" tacked on 35 years later. But for the interior restoration he was limited to the 1882 modifications.

Recovering old appearances was easier said than done. The Old Capitol had undergone extensive alterations in the intervening years. A 1906 fire had badly damaged the Senate chamber and the southeastern corner of the building. Contractors erected a half-dome over the Senate dais to hide where the stained glass window was charred, and they replaced the roof. After World War II, when veteran organizations assumed occupancy, Dakin's castle became a monument to architectural afterthought. The tiered floors in both chambers were flattened, and acoustical tile was suspended from the ceilings. In 1955, contractors added another level to the House chamber, creating a warren of fluorescent cubicles. Meanwhile, the paint scheme kept changing with the payroll. "Every time someone came in that didn't like the color, he changed it," says Kevin Harris, a Baton Rouge architect who later became the state's liaison with McNaughton.[20]

Over the years neglect had taken its toll. In the 1950s and '60s the rotunda was a popular location for LSU fraternity parties. Dakin's fence was an inviting target for vandals. Not long ago one of its cast iron eagles appeared in an antique auction advertisement. "I called offering to buy it," said Bob Courtney, an assistant Secretary of State now in charge of the Old State Capitol. "They said I was welcome to bid on it. I did them one better. I sent the state police over with a warrant and they seized it."[21]

McNaughton assembled a team of experts to investigate the Old Capitol's physical and human history. Scholars examined newspapers, photo collections, and university archives (including James Dakin's construction diary) for clues regarding the building's past appearance. Engineers analyzed the lime and sand content of the mortar and plaster. With the aid of a stereo-zoom binocular microscope, restoration experts used fresh surgeon scalpels to excise samples of original paint for laboratory analysis. McNaughton himself excavated long closed-up turrets. "Climbing a series of ladders in one of the towers," he wrote, "we worked our way above a mechanical equipment space to the attic of the west chamber. . . Window frames on the west wall were charred but still contained remnants of finish and the wood substrate was virtually intact. . . . Working our way over the ceiling joists along the interior walls, we saw construction marks which tell a most interesting tale. The mortar line of the former roof slopes in the opposite direction to the current roof. . . ."[22]

Repairing the glass dome was a large challenge. Twenty percent of the glass panes were missing, and the original pattern had lost coherence due to the haphazard manner in which replacement panes had been inserted over the years. Contractors had hung chicken wire under the dome to catch glass that weekly crashed on the marble floors. Dust filtered out the light. "As the dome got dirtier, the glow got a little dimmer," said Kevin Harris, the Baton Rouge architect. The restoration team ultimately removed, tagged, and cleaned over 2,000 panes of glass, restoring them to their original harlequin design. For replacement panes McNaughton sent away to the Czechoslovakian glass works that had supplied the originals.

To replace doorknobs and decorative bronze hardware, the restoration team scoured an 1879 catalog for original designs and then had them recast. McNaughton even visited a lock museum in Connecticut to track down information. Mennonite cabinetmakers from DeRidder, Louisiana, replicated Gothic millwork according to old catalogs. Dutch wood grainers restained the oak moldings. Nineteenth-century timbers were sawed to preserve the pine flooring's integrity.

Painstaking attention to detail ensured a successful restoration. McNaughton carefully recorded his research team's findings in a thick *Historic Structures Report*, replete with appendices. "In the past, the information on a particular building always remained in the head of the architect," he said. "When he died it was like the crashing of a hard disk or the burning of a library. I wanted to develop a document that another professional could actually use for restoration of this building in the future."

Phase I of the restoration—mainly the exterior work and the glass dome—was completed in 1986. Then the project stopped.

So long as the state was pumping big oil profits from the bayou, getting sufficient funds for renovating the Old State Capitol was a minor concern. After oil prices collapsed in the mid-eighties, however, the money tree lost its foliage. Unemployment skyrocketed. By 1988, the state was struggling to stave off bankruptcy. Every year the Louisiana State Museum Board requested $5 to 6 million to complete the restoration project. But the legislature repeatedly excised Dakin's castle from the capital outlay budget. "We lobbied aggressively for funding for all of our institutions," said Bill Allerton, a board member who worked the legislature on the State Museum's behalf.[23] The un-airconditioned building, however, remained closed until July 1988.

Meanwhile, James Sefcik had been brought in from the State Historical Society of Wisconsin as the new State Museum director. When the state scraped together leftover funds, Sefcik reopened the facility to the public. Long-range use plans envisioned converting the building into a museum on state politics, on the logic that tourists know as much about Louisiana politicians as they do its chefs. Dakin's castle closed a short time later. After high humidity damaged a traveling exhibit, Sefcik advised against resuming full-time operations until the interior renovations had been completed.[24]

The closure alarmed Baton Rouge friends of the Old State Capitol. Although the Louisiana museum system was state-wide in scope, the crown jewels were the Cabildo, Presbytere, and Old Mint in the French Quarter. Not only was the Director based in the city, New

Orleanians dominated the governing board. After a fire gutted the Cabildo in 1988, its restoration commanded most of the Museum Board's resources. In Baton Rouge fear ran high that the Old Capitol project would take a back seat to the Cabildo. Early in 1990, Baton Rouge politicians and preservationists organized to remove the Old Capitol from State Museum Board jurisdiction.

The key player was Brian Kendrick, today a Saks Fifth Avenue vice-president in New York. Before becoming Governor Buddy Roemer's Commissioner of Administration—and setter of budget agendas—Kendrick had been Chief Financial Officer of Baton Rouge's major retail firm. A member of a preservationist group called the Old State Capitol Associates, he had also once chaired the city's Downtown Development District. But the most valuable asset Kendrick brought to the table was his close relationship with the governor. "He was the one man Buddy couldn't say no to," averred Bill Allerton.[25]

Enmity between Baton Rouge business interests and the State Museum Board had been brewing for years. The fights were over local control. Periodically, the Baton Rouge DDD would ask permission to use the Old State Capitol for social functions. "First of all, they found it very repugnant to have to come to New Orleans and bow and scrape to use a building that's in their backyard," said Bill Allerton. "Second, we consistently turned them down because their proposed functions failed to meet nationally-recog-

nized museum guidelines that we had adopted—like how you prepare food in a building. And they would say, 'Goddamn it, we're not going to let these debutantes in New Orleans dictate the use of our building.' That was the centerpiece to their opposition, in my opinion."

An important tactician on the legislative side was Mike Baer, the Secretary of the Louisiana Senate. Baer became a born-again preservationist after Huey Long's bathroom was sledgehammered into oblivion. "It was on the 25th floor of the new capitol," Baer says. "Huey had this stall put in with multiple shower heads. It was just a phenomenal place. One day I went up to inspect the renovations being done at the time. They had destroyed that bathroom. Just torn it totally out. I think that's what woke me up and got me so interested in preservation." After Dakin's Gothic castle was closed to the public for a second time, Baer wanted the legislature to assume control.[26]

In the spring of 1990, Baton Rouge interests determined to transfer the Old Capitol to the Secretary of State's office, headed by Fox McKeithen. The proposal made economic sense because the State Department could fund the Old Capitol from filing and copying fees—a powerful argument to a cash-strapped legislature. McKeithen's office also housed the State Archives, whose functions included museum displays. Proponents of the transfer underscored the Secretary of State's historical

credentials. "Fox grew up listening to Earl Long stories," said Bob Courtney, McKeithen's assistant, "and he truly loves political history. He used to teach history in high school when he coached football in north Louisiana."

The takeover fight was pretty one-sided. State Museum forces were never able to put up much of a struggle. "You have to understand how politics here are done," Baer said. "By the time the legislative committees meet we know what is going to happen." The legislation was steamrollered through the House, despite opposition from the Orleans Parish delegation. Although things became vitriolic in the Senate, the battle there was hardly larger than a skirmish.

In actuality, it was an old-fashioned New Orleans bashing. "We made it an Orleans versus the rest of the state kind of contest. That's the only way we could win it," said Bob Courtney.

Mike Baer talked about the victory the way LSU fans used to gloat over mauling Tulane in football. "This fight was pure, gut politics of taking something from a silk-stocking board down in New Orleans," he said.

Jim Sefcik, the State Museum director, adopted a wry midwestern fatalism about the controversy. "Had I been in their shoes, I might have done the same thing," he said of the new users of the Old State Capitol. "Their job was to make themselves look good. To those guys in Baton Rouge, I was from Wisconsin, so who cares?"

After the Old State Capitol's transfer to Fox McKeithen's office, Phase II restoration money ($6.5 million in all) finally made it into the capital outlay budget.

When Bob Courtney took charge of Phase II renovations, he wasted little time articulating Baton Rouge's expectations for the castle. "The quickest way to kill a building," he explained, "is to adorn it with velvet ropes and glass cases. I don't want any barriers. This is the people's building, and the more they want to use it, the better." But Courtney's insistence that the Old Capitol be made available for social occasions—which, truth to tell, harks back to the original blueprint—was opposed by McNaughton, who represented the "pure" museum perspective.

They wrangled over whether to install a service elevator and build a kitchen. A sharp fight erupted over removing the semi-dome installed above the Senate dais following the 1906 fire. The Secretary of State's office insisted that it come down, to expose the charred alcove.

Phase II restorations were completed in time for the scheduled opening on April 29, 1994—to a fanfare of patriotic speeches, ribbon cutting, martial music, and economic boosterism. The night before, a white tie gathering of big contributors and other notables in the old House chamber heard former governors Dave Treen, Buddy Roemer, and Fox's father John, swap political war stories. Today visitors to the chamber can view a high-tech slide show on Louisiana history, theme music courtesy of "Jurassic Park."

Huey Long never cared for the building. It was the setting of his 1929 impeachment, spearheaded by Standard Oil lawyer Cecil Morgan, whose ancestors once owned the land now occupied by the Old State Capitol. Historians generally agree the abortive impeachment represented a turning point in Huey Long's drive for power. The Kingfish said as much himself: "I used to try to get things done by saying 'please.' That didn't work and now I am a dynamiter. I dynamite 'em out of my path." One thing rumor says he wanted to blow up was the Old State Capitol. Either that, or turn it over to a "collector of antiques."[27] In depression-era Louisiana the Kingfish usually got his way, but fortunately not in this instance. Maybe it was because he was in a hurry to erect his own monument to power and beauty.

A circular staircase in the Old State Capitol leads to the second floor in the building's rotunda. Gold leaf, widely applied during the building's 1994 restoration, enhances the capitol's neo-Gothic beauty and Victorian elegance. Architect William A. Freret also used gold leaf during the 1880s renovations.

The spiral staircase winds toward the stained glass, interior dome in the Old State Capitol's fully restored rotunda.

A solitary podium rests on the stage of the fully restored House of Representatives chamber. The chamber is intended for public forums as the Louisiana Center for Political History.

The rotunda and staircase are
seen from near the ceiling in
the Old State Capitol.

THE GOVERNORS OF LOUISIANA

Visitors to the Old State Capitol view a computerized video image of William C.C. Claiborne in the exhibit hall. Claiborne was first American territorial governor appointed by President Thomas Jefferson after the Louisiana Purchase in 1803. He presided over what was then called the Territory of Orleans, now the state of Louisiana. The state elected Claiborne its first governor after its admission to the Union in 1812.

A video image of former Governor Earl Long and the text of his speech flank a podium in the Old State Capitol's exhibit hall. In his speech Earl Long describes items that are taxed in Texas but are spared in Louisiana. From the interactive podium, visitors can select excerpts of speeches by various Louisiana politicians. The large photograph behind the podium shows clerks being sworn in for the Huey Long impeachment trial in the Old State Capitol's Senate chamber.

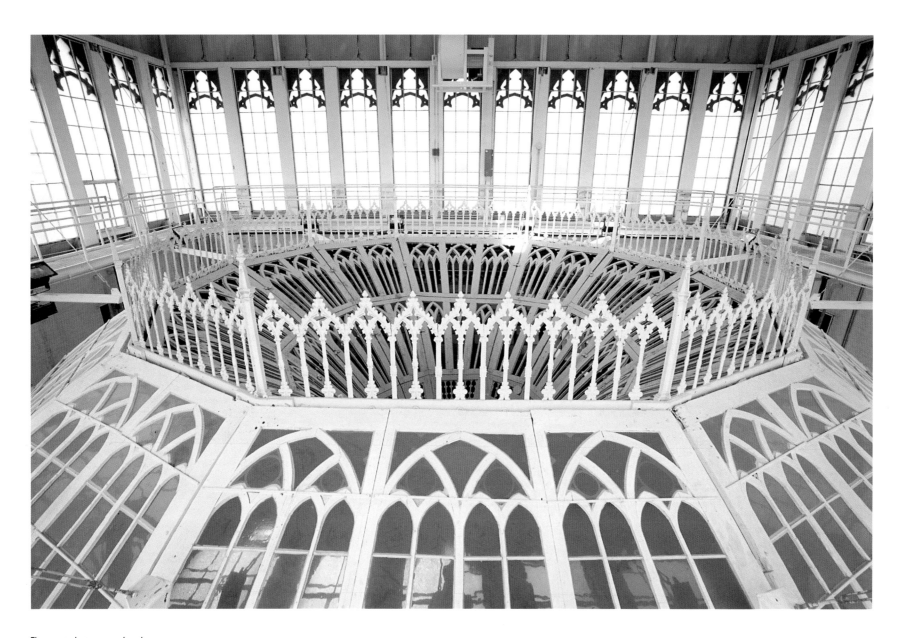

The ornate lantern covering the
stained glass dome above the
Capitol's rotunda suggests a 19th-
century riverboat pilot house. It was
added on to the Capitol by William
Freret during the 1880s renovations.

Turrets on the roof of the Old State
Capitol stand guard over the
Mississippi River bridge and the U.S.S.
Kidd, a World War II destroyer.

The Old State Capitol from the
southeast at dusk

Interior light illuminates the House
chamber's stained glass window of
the neo-Gothic structure.

Construction workers' helmets hang
on the fence surrounding the Old State
Capitol during its 1994 restoration.

Robert Reilly, on-site curator for the Old State Capitol, inspects the building's restoration in 1992. He retired later that year.

Light filtered through stained glass strikes the false floor of the House chamber during the building's most recent restoration. The false floor was installed after the state government vacated the Old State Capitol in 1932. In the ensuing years, the room served primarily as office space.

Construction workers examine the House chamber's original tiered floor after removing the false floor during restoration. The three channels in the floor had been cut out for air conditioning ducts and sprinklers.

Stained glass windows filter the
light on Tommy Mack, a plasterer,
during restoration.

Claire Van der Klemp, of Holland, applies a faux bois stain to cypress molding giving it the appearance of more expensive oak. All the woodwork on the building is original to the 1882 restoration.

In front of the Senate chamber's
stained glass window, exposed
beams show how the window's top
was concealed after a fire in 1906.

Mike Creel installs a false ceiling
support grid above the Senate
chamber's stained glass window
making it fully visible. The brick
wall is original to the building's
1849 construction.

Secretary of State W. Fox
McKeithen waves an Old State
Capitol promotional fan during a
media event announcing a
donation for the restoration by
ARCO Chairman Lod Cook.

Secretary of State W. Fox
McKeithen addresses the audience
in the fully renovated House of
Representatives chamber during
the Old State Capitol's grand
opening gala on April 29, 1994.

Former Louisiana Governors Buddy
Roemer, Dave Treen, and John
McKeithen prepare themselves for
a televised forum in the Old State
Capitol during its grand opening.

Former Governor John McKeithen laughs with colleagues during the often humorous forum at the Old State Capitol's grand opening.

Guests mingle in the Senate chamber during the Old State Capitol's grand opening gala. Restorations fully revealed the stained glass window seen in the background.

Celebrants at the Old State Capitol's
grand opening gala gather around
the rotunda staircase.

U.S. Senator John Breaux cuts a ribbon at the public grand opening of the restored Old State Capitol on April 30, 1994. This date is the anniversary of Louisiana statehood in 1812, and the signing of the Louisiana Purchase in 1803.

A military honor guard climbs the
steps to the Old State Capitol
during grand opening ceremonies.

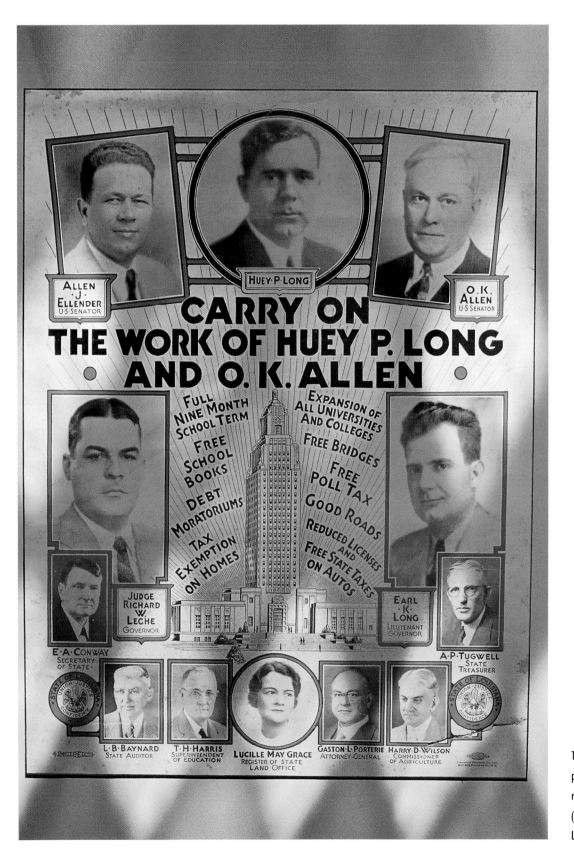

This 1936 gubernatorial campaign poster for Judge Richard Leche represents the legacy of Longism. (Opposite page) Office door handle, Louisiana State Capitol

MONUMENTS AND MEMORY

Solis Seiferth was fond of recalling how
Weiss, Dreyfous & Seiferth became project
architects for Huey Long's Art Deco skyscraper. Leon C. Weiss, the firm's senior
partner and chief rainmaker, was sitting next
to the Governor during dedication ceremonies
for a New Orleans furniture store. The two
men had never met before. In fact, nobody
from Weiss, Dreyfous & Seiferth (pronounced
Seefert) had even supported Long in the 1928
gubernatorial election. Huey leaned over and
mentioned he had dreamed for a long time
about building a new state capitol. "I may
want to talk to you and get your suggestions
about an architect," he said. "How about
somebody from my office," Weiss replied.
The quick response brought the firm its most
important contract. In those days the Kingfish
was the Selection Board.[1]

Most people still think of Huey Long as a
demagogue and a true friend of the poor. He
earned the reputation during the Great Depression while rallying a mass movement called

Share-the-Wealth, which advocated limiting
great fortunes. In Louisiana the Kingfish's
record is somewhat spotty. He provided free
textbooks and medical care. LSU became a lot
more accessible to poor students than in the
past. But Huey hardly soaked the rich. Standard Oil footed most of the bill, and then
passed it along to out-of-state gas consumers.

Huey's performance as governor was most
consistent in the realm of bricks and mortar.

His free bridges and paved roads literally
brought Louisiana out of the mud. The
Kingfish also constructed buildings—a lot of
them.[2] The structure in which he took
greatest pride was the new state capitol,
completed in 1932. He contrasted its moder-
nity with the antiquated castle, bragging that
his skyscraper could accommodate all the
departments of state government. As much as
anything, he liked the building's verticality.
In its time the Art Deco structure was the
South's tallest building. "The idea of a
skyscraper was entirely Huey Long's,"
Seiferth recalled. Long wanted a structure
that would loom over the flat landscape.

Although Huey described himself as *sui
generis*, his edifice complex was hardly out of
the ordinary. Monumental architecture has
always attracted politicians and rulers. This
was a period when Hitler laid plans to construct a vast House of the People in Berlin
(capacious enough on paper to contain three
Superdomes), and Stalin envisioned erecting

soaring wedding cake palaces.[3] Triumphal buildings symbolize power and effectiveness, if only because their construction provides employment to jobless millions. During the 1930s, public projects showed bewildered masses that great men could defy economic calamity. It was a mark of Huey's genius that he grasped this political principle long before most other leaders of his time.

Decked in a purple shirt and white suit, his auburn hair crowned with a straw hat, the Kingfish lived life at breakneck speed. "He had a fantastic drive," Seiferth said of his most famous client. "I mean he wanted everything immediately. He seemed to have a premonition that something was going to happen."

Huey's drive was crucial to obtaining the construction money for the new capitol. Thanks to opposition from the New Orleans Old Regulars or "Choctaws," the 1930 legislature initially stymied the capitol bond issue. Long responded by running that summer for the U.S. Senate. Huey's inroads into the city vote cut so deeply that the "Choctaws" reversed their position in a special session of the legislature. The Kingfish brushed aside conservative diehards, drilling a hole in the ceiling above an opponent's desk to let rain water pour through. Huey's younger brother Earl tried sabotaging the funding bill, too, saying the proposed capitol looked like a "farm silo." The Kingfish drove the legislation to passage on September 18, 1930. Construction commenced shortly before Christmas.[4]

Aside from insisting the project stay within budget, Huey seldom intervened in the construction itself. He never startled watchmen late at night to inspect the structure inch by inch, as happened earlier during the construction of the governor's mansion.[5] "He left us strictly alone on things that he didn't know about," Seiferth said. Long's hands-off policy gave the architects tremendous latitude with the new capitol.

Weiss, Dreyfous & Seiferth, who extensively studied other state capitols, were greatly influenced by Bertram Goodhue's masterful Nebraska State Capitol, the first successful attempt to fit a public building into an American skyscraper.[6] The three New Orleans architects, however, came up with a different motif for their tower. Critics call it "beaux arts modernism" or Art Deco, in reference to a Jazz Age style that left its stamp on furniture, cigarette lighters, and—in Louisiana—the seat of government. The building's "beaux arts" are also visible in its large sunken park—a carryover from the "city beautiful" movement—and its symmetrical massing. The tower's ziggurat set-backs, the matching block wings, the repeating geometry, all suggested the dynamism of modern life.[7] At the same time, as Weiss, Dreyfous and Seiferth explained to Governor Long, the structure exuded "the atmosphere, or feeling, of the classic, tending toward the Greek influence."[8]

Huey laid down one other condition. As Seiferth put it, "everything had to be done fast." Huey wanted the building finished by the time he left for Washington in January,

1932, to be sworn in as U.S. Senator. That gave the architects slightly more than a year to complete the project. State capitols in America have never been erected quickly. Because of local politics Goodhue's Nebraska tower took a dozen years to build.[9] Huey's skyscraper was finished in fourteen months.

By the start of 1931, the construction site on the old LSU campus, next to the Baton Rouge levee, was crawling with heavy equipment. George A. Fuller & Company, the Washington-based firm that had won the construction contract, built a pile-testing yard for the 1,900 reinforced concrete piles that were sunk on the premises. A railroad spur brought in 2,500 carloads of stone, steel, and marble. So frenetic was the pace, caterpillars bulldozed not only a campus but a Spanish-era cemetery as well. A plaintiff's attorney threatened legal action because, as he explained to the architects, "the body of a relative of my clients was dug up by a steam shovel, cut in half, badly mutilated, and thrown upon the dump surrounding the Capitol building."

The New Orleans offices of Weiss, Dreyfous & Seiferth were just as active. "I've always found that architecture is more or less feast or famine," Seiferth reminisced late in life. The capitol project was a veritable banquet. The firm hired fifty draftsmen to draw up detailed plans for everything from door knobs to bathroom fixtures. A blizzard of drawings and specification sheets blew from their desks: 20,000 blueprints, 80,000 mimeo sheets, squalls of notes and letters.[10] "It was a fantastic job keeping an office like that going," Seiferth said.

Meanwhile the 34-story building rose inexorably against the mirrored image spreading across the capitol reflecting lake. By late May, 1931, six months after the groundbreaking, the foundation and base of Huey's monument had been completed. Six weeks later a steel skeletal tower was in place. Six weeks after that the building's limestone exterior had reached the sixteenth floor.

If one person at Weiss, Dreyfous & Seiferth deserves major credit for driving the project through to completion, it is Leon C. Weiss, the senior partner. Educated at Tulane, Weiss died in 1953 before recording his own reminiscences of events, but his firm's voluminous correspondence leaves no doubt about his role. Weiss was a tireless perfectionist—with a sense of humor. But in official photographs he wears a grim, single-minded visage.

There is no question Weiss looked on the project as the job of a lifetime. Rising early, he labored late dashing off letters and telegrams. Sometimes he worked all night. One week he was on a train to New York; another week, to Washington; then New York again. Meanwhile, there was the ceaseless crawling back and forth over the primitive roads linking Baton Rouge and New Orleans. One evening, after a busy week in the northeast, he wrote an eight page letter from the Mayflower Hotel in Washington to his partners in New Orleans

concerning project business, after which he collapsed from exhaustion: "I must get to bed. I am tired and it is nearly 1:00 a.m."[11]

Building Huey's capitol required patience as well. For political reasons the $5 million capitol construction budget had been divided among nearly every bank in Louisiana. An ingenious method of propping up the state's teetering banking industry, the practice also consolidated Long's political base. But it also meant pro rating requisitions among numerous accounts all over the state. Complaints about late payment poured in constantly.

Toughness came with the job, too. When a Fuller Company vice-president wrote asking for a 20-day schedule extension because of late payment by the state, Weiss replied: "this is the most baseless claim for extension that we have ever had made upon us during our many years of practice." He denied the request.[12]

A different set of skills was necessary for dealing with the capitol's artists and sculptors: tact and diplomacy. The original plans envisioned very little architectural ornamentation. But when major construction bids came in unexpectedly low, due to the depression, Weiss, Dreyfous & Seiferth decided to etch Louisiana flora and history onto Huey's monument and bedeck it with statuary. For the task they assembled several of the best architectural sculptors working in America at the time: the Chicago sculptor, Lorado Taft; German émigré Ulric Ellerhusen; Adolph Weinman; Lee Lawrie; and Angela Gregory, a young Newcomb College professor just begin-

ning to acquire a national reputation.[13]

One problem Weiss faced with the sculptors was their resistance to being hurried. "This rushing the work through is very costly to me," Ellerhusen said, after being prodded to hasten progress on the historical friezes he was designing for the building's fifth floor. "It is a catastrophe," replied Lorado Taft to Weiss' insistence that the plaster models for the sculpture groups flanking the stairs be shipped immediately. "As I foresaw, the job is costing me all that I get for it." Weiss tried responding with cajolery and flattery. The stone had to be quarried, blocked out, cut, and shipped on tight schedule, he told the artists. The steel framing was going up apace. And, as the architect intimated more than once, the hot breath of Huey's impatience was breathing down his neck. Weiss persuaded the Kingfish to postpone the dedication twice. But in view of interminable delays, there was still no guarantee the latest deadline would be met, and he was worried.[14]

Weiss was usually good at smoothing over small contractual disagreements with his sculptors.[15] With Lee Lawrie, probably the most famous of the group, diplomacy broke down completely. The firm had commissioned him to do the main entrance portal, together with the figures on the tower temple, and it paid him what he asked, without question. Although the relationship began well, it quickly unraveled due to missed deadlines. Four months into the project Lawrie suspended work, complaining he had yet to receive a signed contract. The work stoppage held up 80 carloads of stone waiting to be hung on the steel skeleton. "You can see what a jam we are in," Weiss wrote in exasperation.

As the project neared completion Lawrie was slow getting plaster models to the stone carvers at the building site. Weiss wired that the latest delay was causing monetary losses, "besides producing an extremely disagreeable and annoying situation" (he had just convinced Huey to postpone the dedication). He also alleged Lawrie had allowed other studio projects to take precedence over Huey's capitol. "Your telegram is not truthful nor in a proper tone," the sculptor replied. Weiss issued a warning: "When you bandy the word liar in a letter, you are stepping on our toes and might arouse a resentment which you would regret."[16]

One cause of friction was the firm's attention to detail. They wanted their building engraved not only with Louisiana flora and fauna but a chronicle of the state's evolution from primordial ooze to modern leviathan. Weiss' two partners, Julius Dreyfous and Solis Seiferth, were responsible for researching indigenous animal and plant life. They were sticklers about approving every sketch. The interlacing cane motif on the window panels was "stiff and ugly," they complained about the bronze panel doors in Memorial Hall. Change it. The hurricane scene shows erect trees that should be wind-blown. Bend them down. The bent left leg on Governor Henry W. Allen's statue gives "an unhappy effect." The

hand of one of the casket girls in Ellerhusen's frieze was "rather. . . oversized." The architects scribbled commentary upon hundreds of drawings and photographs.[17]

Instead of producing tedium, the detail leads to fun and mirth. On the "governor only" elevator door, pelicans devour frogs. Crawfish, raccoons, and mink lurk in the window panels. Crabs and turtles nest in the marbled cat-tails atop Tuscan columns. Even conventional symbology is flavored with Louisiana drollery. Over the entrance to the Louisiana Senate chamber a Roman fasces is partly enveloped by bronze kudzu. And so on through a zoological and botanical phylum of egrets, eagles, sugarcane, cotton, corn, magnolias, and marsh grass. Arranged against richly colored marble, the intricate Louisiana motifs bring a grin. It is as though Louisiana's emperor was setting his circus.

If buildings hold memory, Weiss, Dreyfous & Seiferth were determined that Huey's monument carry the right history lessons. Dreyfous and Seiferth, who researched this subject, mailed book excerpts and bibliographical citations to out-of-state sculptors. Henry P. Dart, a New Orleans lawyer and legal scholar, even conducted crash courses over lunch about the Louisiana civil law tradition.[18]

Not surprisingly, the history lesson was oriented to the Crescent City. Twelve of the twenty-two faces chiseled above the exterior windows of the House and Senate chambers

are New Orleanians. City personalities and references dominate the Civil War images in Ellerhusen's historical friezes. The same is true of the scene used to depict "Louisiana at Play": Rex and his krewe passing in front of New Orleans street revelers.[19]

Weiss, Dreyfous & Seiferth had difficulty dealing with Reconstruction, however. In the 1930s, conventional wisdom about the period was steeped in white supremacy. The firm intended to bronze likenesses of former governors onto the main elevator doors, but it winced at including Reconstruction rulers. Henry Clay Warmoth, the first carpetbagger governor, had been demonized by historians. P.B.S. Pinchback, the country's only black governor to that point in time, had fared even worse. The firm asked Henry Dart for advice. Although Dart's racial attitudes were archconservative, the New Orleans attorney believed in historical veracity. Warmoth's administration rivalled in importance William C.C. Claiborne's, the first governor, Dart explained. And, he added, Pinchback's tenure, while brief, had been recognized by Congress and the U. S. Supreme Court. "The truth of history requires all or none," Dart intoned, and he saw no recourse but to include them all.[20]

The New Orleans architects respected Dart's advice. The phrase about history requiring all or none is "practically unanswerable," Seiferth conceded. Nonetheless his firm chose to sacrifice truth to conventional wisdom. "We have . . . shown all, with the exception of Pinchback," the architect continued. As for Warmoth, they decided to stuff him onto a panel with four other Reconstruction-era governors" a happy solution," Seiferth explained, "as it properly subordinated them and still preserved the continuity and full truth of history."[21]

Huey interfered only once in the historical sermonizing, when he complained about Lorado Taft's original design for the "Pioneers" grouping. He objected to the large cross in the foreground and ordered it removed. Long told Weiss that his capitol should be "non-sectarian and inoffensive to any class or creed of the citizenry of the State." After playing with the idea of substituting a book or "some highly significant vegetable," the sculptor finally settled on an open Bible, which was accepted.[22]

Except for that ecumenical gesture, Huey's hand was scarcely to be seen. The architects could not even persuade him to slow down long enough to pose for a photograph Ellerhusen needed for a frieze panel.[23]

As it happened, the architects had to postpone the building's dedication until May 16, 1932, too late for Huey to attend. At the time of the capitol's unveiling, the Kingfish was on the U.S. Senate floor filibustering a deficit reduction tax bill, quoting Daniel Webster and other 19th-century giants about the dangers of economic inequality in a democracy.[24]

Huey's building is beginning to shift. Several steps bearing the names of states are threatening secession. Recently, inspectors discovered that during the hasty construction steel rods had been omitted from some stone slabs. "The Capitol is not going to fall down tomorrow," says Charles Schwing, the building's current architect, "but without the right kind of attention it will fall in time."[25]

As with the old capitol, Huey's tower hasn't fared well at the hands of critics. The needle skyscraper design has drawn fire, due to the uneconomical use of space. The architectural sculpturing, which changing tastes and tighter finances long ago rendered a lost art, have struck some reviewers as overly busy and distracting. Two architectural historians even say the Travertine-floored Great Memorial Hall has "the sleek improbable Art Deco chic of a Chicago night club."[26]

Because they were placed too high on the building to be seen by the naked eye, Ulric Ellerhusen's historical friezes have been largely ignored. But the lack of visibility may not matter much in the end. The history lesson most people today associate with Huey's capitol wasn't carved by stone cutters but an assassin's bullets. Just behind the elevators in the Great Memorial Hall, next to a Tuscan column crawling with crabs and alligators, are several large bullet holes. The gougings in the Levanto marble wall are the main tourist attraction in Huey's capitol.[27]

The Kingfish had prophesied the Long inner circle would probably end up in jail without his controlling presence. Several associates ultimately did go to prison as a result of the Louisiana Hayride scandals. One person caught in the net was Leon C. Weiss, convicted in 1939 of mail fraud for alleged construction irregularities at Louisiana Tech University in north Louisiana. He served two years in a federal penitentiary.[28] Because the trial was held in Shreveport, there are rumors Weiss was the victim of an upstate vendetta against New Orleans, if not anti-semitism (Weiss was Jewish). One of his daughters believes he was guilty of naiveté. "My father was a very spiritual and idealistic person," she says.[29]

Confronting the skyscraper capitol is a larger-than-life statue of the Kingfish. It sits in the middle of a French formal garden. Faces of adulatory followers peer skyward from the chiseled stone. Erected in 1940 with a $50,000 legislative appropriation, the monument marks the spot where Huey is buried. Russell Long, Huey's oldest son, and now retired from his father's old U.S. Senate seat, posed for the statue.[30]

Before the Kingfish's advent an oligarchy of big planters, corporate lawyers, and the New Orleans machine ran the state like a closely-held business. By delivering real goods and services and showing he could defeat the depression, Huey recast state politics for three generations. To remain competitive, anti-Longites learned to preach honesty and efficiency instead of fiscal conservatism. After Huey there was no turning back the clock to the days of do-nothing government.[31]

A key ingredient of Longite populism was a plenitude of mineral wealth. Oil and gas profits kept taxes low and services high, endowing the governor with extraordinary patronage. They also shielded most homeowners from property taxes. Voters winked at the corruption since they never had to pick up the tab.[32] The mid-eighties oil bust, coupled with declining middle-class opportunity, dissolved the Longite social contract. As budget deficits soared, Louisiana tax payers have gone into revolt. Conservatives are once again calling for minimalist government. Huey's protégés have turned to legalized gambling as the new cash cow, but its revenues will never replace mineral royalties. For the first time in living memory Louisiana politics has become a bitter struggle over how to slice a shrinking pie.

The Louisiana legislature is showing strains of the transition. "In the old days, there was a camaraderie, there was a love, there was an affection," says Senate secretary Mike Baer, who arrived in the capitol in 1972. "Those days are gone. Now, they get on the mike and call each other liars. They call each other dirty names."

When the legislature is not wrangling over abortion, it is fighting endless battles over how to raise taxes, where to cut spending, where to look for new revenue. Louisiana lobbyists— the so-called "axperts" and street smart country boys hired on contract by business interests— complain of legislative Machiavellianism. "You win a few, you lose a few, and sometimes the umpire steals a few," one lobbyist was overheard muttering to a colleague outside a packed Senate Finance Committee hearing during the 1993 regular session.

According to columnist John Maginnis, Governor Edwin Edwards is as much a part of the state capitol as the bullet holes. In 1994, however, he announced his retirement from politics after four terms in the governor's mansion. Edwards governed best when dishing out patronage, contracts, and witty candor. Now that the treasury is running on empty, voters snarl instead of chuckle. His departure represents the passing of a political era.[33]

Mike Baer believes even the merriment is disappearing. The non-stop parties at local hotels during legislative sessions have shut down. "You used to walk into one of the hotel lounges, and there'd be laughing and joking and hollering and drinking," said Baer. "Then we'd go cook squirrel head stew at midnight, and stay up till two a.m. every morning." The next day festivities continued with three and four martini lunches. "You could always tell how successful lunch was by the quality of oratory that afternoon," says Baer. But the hotels have closed and the lawmakers have cut back on the drinking for health reasons. "We go in at 1:30, nobody's drunk, they walk out on the floor cold sober, and it's boring as hell."

It's hard to escape feeling that an epoch in state politics has started to vanish. Not long ago Andrei Codrescu, a Romanian writer and LSU professor, reminded listeners in wry commentary for National Public Radio how Huey's capitol harked back to a bygone era. "The other day I woke up in the Soviet Union," he said. "It doesn't happen very often, but there it was. The tall forties-style building that could have been the I.V. Stalin Typographical Union. The statue of Molotov with the adoring masses crawling up his sides. The industrial haze that turned everything the color of lead."[34]

Codrescu broadcast his *déjà vu* sensations before the collapse of the Soviet Union, but that only amplifies their relevance. Nowadays one gets the impression that the Old Regime in Louisiana is likewise passing from the stage of history. Huey's skyscraper stands as that epoch's most striking symbol. But in its assertion of power, its Social Realism, its Art Deco idealism, its refinery-begrimed surfaces, Long's monument seems almost out of time.

Ironically, the hard-scrabbled poverty that propelled the Kingfish's rise to power has not disappeared. It has simply been shunted across the landscape.

Capitol Lake north of
the State House

Capitol at dawn with the Mississippi
River in the distance

Capitol at midday

Petrochemical refineries illuminate
the darkening sky behind the
State Capitol.

Front staircase to the Capitol

An Evangeline-like figure in the
"The Pioneers" cluster sculpted by
Lorado Taft

An angel representing the Spirit of
Law rests atop the Capitol Tower
on one corner of the building.
Three other angels representing the
Spirits of Philosophy, Art and
Science grace the other corners.

"The Patriots" cluster stands in front of the Capitol. Both "The Patriots" and "The Pioneers" pay tribute to those who settled and later defended Louisiana. Lorado Taft sculpted the figures.

A frontal view of
"The Patriots" cluster

Adolph Weinman's frieze "Government
Based on Law, Order, and Justice
Fostering the Higher Aspirations of the
People" graces the Capitol's front wall
to the left of the main doors.

A frieze entitled "The Spirit of
Liberty and Peace Furthering the
Material Welfare of the People" by
Adolph A. Weinman stands to the
right of the Capitol's entrance.

A frieze of Andrew Jackson leading the Battle of New Orleans is part of a mural that wraps around the top of the Capitol's base at the fifth floor level. Sculpted by Ulric Ellerhusen, the mural illustrates Louisiana history and life. Unfortunately much of it is obscured from view by the two legislative chambers on each side of the Capitol's tower. To see it in detail, one needs binoculars.

A detail from the Ellerhusen mural
depicts Mardi Gras in New Orleans.
This part of the mural is also out
of view from the ground.

This detail from the architrave surrounding the Capitol's front portal suggests the compatibility of nature's bounty and heavy industry. The sculptor is Lee Lawrie.

Sculpted fishermen raise nets on the architrave surrounding the main entrance to the Capitol. Lee Lawrie sculpted the work.

A solitary American Indian is sculpted
into a wall behind the Capitol.

A portion of Ulric Ellerhusen's mural depicts the history of Louisiana's judiciary on the Capitol's north wall. The word "confidence" is part of state motto "Union, Justice, Confidence."

In Memorial Hall, some of Louisiana's earliest governors are sculpted on the elevator doors used by staff and visitors alike. The Piccarilli Brothers studio in New York sculpted the Governors' faces.

A state employee peers from an office window at the front of the Capitol. To her left and right are friezes symbolizing the four dominions of Louisiana: Spain, The United States, The Confederacy, and France. The sculptor is Lee Lawrie.

Lobbyists enter the Capitol through a stained glass doorway entitled "Louisiana Aquatica". Baton Rouge artist Stephen Wilson installed the work in 1984. The Capitol's art deco style inspired this gift of the Mc Ilhenny family.

Above the activity in Memorial Hall reigns the goddess of knowledge in a mural "The Abundance of the Earth". Painted by Jules Guerin, the goddess holds a zodiac and an hourglass in her outstretched hands.

GALVEZ APPEALS TO THE LOUISIANIANS – 1779

On this Senate door Spanish Colonial Governor Bernardo Galvez appeals to Louisianians gathered at Place d'Armes (now Jackson Square) to fight the British during the American Revolutionary War. Fifty such friezes of Louisiana historical scenes cover the House and Senate doors.

Assistant Sergeant at Arms Louis Walker guards the Representatives' entrance to the House chamber. The door's top panel depicts the Old State Capitol, while the second shows the Confederate State House in Shreveport used after Union troops captured Baton Rouge during the Civil War.

The railing around the bronzed
relief map of Louisiana serves as a
gathering place in Memorial Hall.

Art Deco motifs of egrets and crabs
adorn the state employees' elevator
in the back hall of the Capitol.

Holes mark the site of Huey Long's assassination in the corridor behind Memorial Hall. Debate persists six decades afterwards as to whether these are actually bullet holes or simply defects in the marble.

Huey Long's statue over his grave
faces the Capitol. Charles Keck
scuplted the statue five years after
Long's untimely death.

The base of the Huey Long statue
shows two aspects of his political
legacy, the Capitol itself and one of
many bridges he built in the state.

Huey Long stands among his
followers in this view of the
statue's base.

Flowers placed at Huey Long's grave commemorate the centennial of his birth. The card's inscription reads, "In loving memory, 'Kingfish', Happy 100th birthday. Forget the uh [deduct] box. Who the hell shot ya?"

In the Senate chamber former U.S. Senator Russell Long reminisces about his father on the centennial of Huey Long's birth in 1893.

Governor Edwin Edwards hosts a
luncheon at the Governor's Mansion
prior to addressing a special session
of the legislature.

Before the courtly pose of France's King Louis XIV, Governor Edwin Edwards addresses a task force on violent crime in the Capitol's press room.

Governor Edwards receives a standing
welcome from House and Senate
members in the House chamber
before addressing the legislature.

Governor Edwards waits to address the legislature at the House Speaker's podium. To his left are Senate President Sammy Nunez and House Speaker John Alario.

Governor Edwards addresses a House/Senate conference committee during a budgetary crisis. Without being asked about his casual attire, he explained that he expected the "blood to fly" before he left the tense hearing and saw no point in ruining a good suit. Commissioner of Administration Raymond Laborde sits to his right.

Governor Edwards announces to the
legislature that he would not seek
a fifth term as governor.

Protesters picket against lowering the state's $75,000 homestead exemption on property tax.

Louisiana State Troopers guard the Capitol steps as LSU students and faculty protest proposed budget cuts. The Capitol's steps are so structurally stressed that large crowds can no longer gather on them.

LSU students peer into a House
committee hearing room while
LSU Chancellor William "Bud"
Davis testifies against budget cuts
to the university.

Senator Jim Cox and colleagues
gather for an informal meeting
of the legislature.

Longest serving senator, B.B. "Sixty"
Rayburn stands in a back hallway of
the Capitol.

Representative Jimmy Dimos
visits with House colleagues
prior to a session.

Senators B.B. "Sixty" Rayburn and John Hainkel debate at the Senate floor microphone. By Senate tradition, all questioning and debate is done face to face over the same microphone at the front of the chamber.

Representative Melvin "Kip" Holden
works the telephones at his desk in
the House chamber.

David Duke extends his hand to
fellow Representative Odon
Bacque, the only person who
spoke out against Duke's
admission to the House in 1989.
Bacque refused his handshake.

Members of the Black Caucus
discuss pending legislation with
House Speaker Pro Tempore
Sherman Copelin (bottom center).

Senate President Sammy
Nunez confers with colleagues
at his podium.

House Speaker John Alario talks
with reporter Marsanne Goldsby
in Memorial Hall.

House Appropriations Committee
Chairman Elias "Bo" Ackal confers
with Senate budget staffers.

Senator Don Kelly listens to debate
on the Senate floor.

103

Representative Paulette Irons
casts her vote.

Votes are tallied on an electronic
board behind the Speaker's podium
in the House of Representatives.

Lieutenant Governor Melinda Schwegmann's office door reflects the Capitol as she leaves the Pentagon Barracks.

Louisiana State Treasurer Mary
Landrieu talks with a constituent
in the Senate chambers.

Representatives Jack Smith
and Wilfred Pierre listen
to committee testimony.

An Audubon print of the
Louisiana state bird hangs above
Representative Ted Haik in a
committee hearing room.

Lobbyists in the Senate chamber

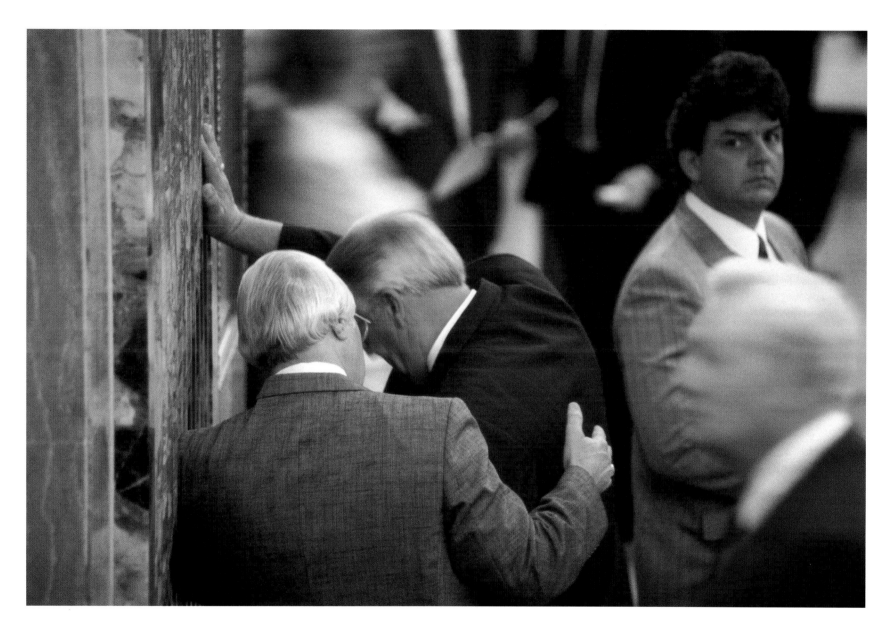

With his hand against the
antechamber wall, a Representative
listens to a lobbyist.

House Speaker Pro Tempore Sherman
Copelin, Jr. and Ed McNeill of the
New Orleans Tourist and Convention
Commission confer in a hallway.

A group of women prepare
requests to lobby Representatives
in the House antechamber.

Receptions for legislators are held on
many evenings in the Pentagon
Barracks and around town. This
particular event was sponsored by the
Louisiana Pest Control Association.

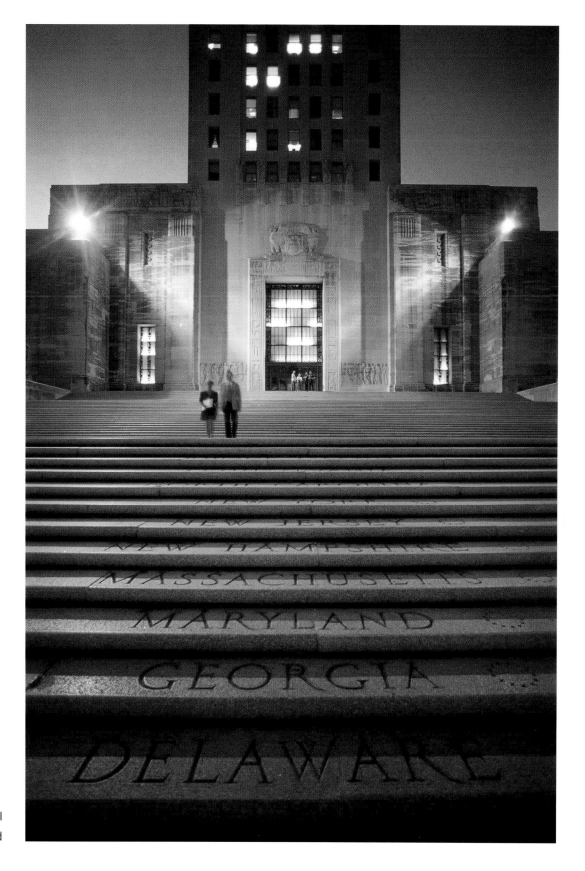

Front steps of the Capitol
at a day's end

"King" Bill Noonan of the Krewe of Bamboozers waves from a float in the Spanish Town Mardi Gras Parade. Crowds watch parachutists (opposite page) on Fourth of July near the Old State Capitol.

EVERY MAN A KING

When Edwin W. Edwards led two jumbo-jets full of supporters to France in 1984, he went with regal ambitions. "I always thought as a child that one day I would become a king, and tonight I can be," he told hundreds of high-rolling contributors.

Each supporter had paid $10,000 for the trip, to help eliminate the debt of America's most expensive gubernatorial election. Wearing "Sun King" lapel pins bearing Edwards' profile, the retinue followed EWE on a Gallic tour that was more carnival parade than junket. Motoring down the moonlit Champs Elysees, bus loads of legislators sang "Jolie Blonde," followed by "You Are My Sunshine." They attended a sumptuous banquet at the Palace of Versailles, Louis XIV's monument to high camp, served by candelabra-bearing waiters in period costume. Hopping between tables in Louie's dining hall, "King" EWE posed in a waiter's periwig as onlookers snapped pictures.

Edwards, the Cajun Pentecostal, is Huey Long's most successful understudy. But he may have outshone his mentor in raising governance to a performance art.

If the original Sun King awed his subjects with resplendence, his Gulf South nephew, like Huey and Earl and other Louisiana populists, has reigned through repartee.

"Governor, I'm going to give you a French kiss," a Louisiana nun living in Paris told Edwards as he exited Notre Dame Cathedral.

"Okay, Sister, just don't let me get in the habit."

When CBS News asked Edwards on camera what the most important thing was that he got from the trip, he quipped, "Five million dollars."

Edwards' governance style is a byproduct of a political culture where campaigns and carnival have become practically synonymous. In the Bayou State the pleasurable is political, and vice versa.[1]

Unlike Bourbon France, where the nobility used the pre-Lenten festival as a social valve for releasing peasant discontent, the Louisiana carnival tradition has long been boisterously democratic. The performance comes from the bottom up no less than the top down. It is a chance for the people to talk back.

Not long after Edwards' Parisian fling, Baton Rouge revelers offered their own take on the governor-elect's fund-raiser. Riding on impromptu floats and in sawed-off Volkswagen Beetles, they cruised through Baton Rouge's Spanish Town, tossing handfuls of "Beaucoup Bucks" bearing pictures of EWE and Huey's capitol to spectators lining the route. Citizens of other American commonwealths express popular consent by pulling levers. Louisianians throw a parade, to let officials know what is really on their mind, for better or worse.

Spanish Town is one of the few parts of Baton Rouge where Mardi Gras satire could have found a beachhead. Lying in the shadow of Huey's capitol, the neighborhood is a strange mix of bohemians and LSU students, plus Cajuns, Italians, and fading remnants of the old merchant class. Vestiges of the original Islénos (Canary Islanders) give the neighborhood its name. "I used to joke that Spanish Town was the northernmost outpost of the Caribbean, what with its shotgun houses and banana trees and wrap-around porches," says Washington-based folklorist Nick Spitzer, who was living in the community at the time. "That Mediterranean littoral ended right there on the capitol grounds." Spitzer, who was studying Creole carnival traditions in south Louisiana, believed Baton Rouge's Anglo intensity needed an infusion of New Orleans mirth. So, in 1981, he and Don Zeringue, an architect now living in St. Francisville, organized the first Spanish Town Mardi Gras. Two years later they persuaded Toyota dealer Price LeBlanc, a fixture on Baton Rouge television, to be king. He threw country sausage to the crowds, which was a trademark of

his car deals (and a throwback to the French carnival tradition "of the wealthy throwing their meat into the street," Spitzer says.)[2]

Spanish Town, whose cemetery rests beneath the capitol, is saturated in Kingfish lore. Huey's assassin Dr. Carl Weiss used to live there, as did some of the Long bodyguards who gunned him down. Castro Carazo, the LSU band director who wrote the music for Huey's "Every Man a King," was still residing in the neighborhood when the first parade rolled. Next to the door bell to his house, a sign read: "Professor Carazo. Music Lessons. Five Dollars an Hour." The second year Spitzer and Zeringue titled the parade "Every Man a Mardi Gras King (and Queen)," beginning a tradition of topical themes. With Huey's capitol as proscenium and prop, the parade circled Long's statue.

From the outset Spanish Town Mardi Gras mixed ribaldry with protest. In the first parade local gays, dressed as pirates in tutus, built a float to mock the destroyer *U.S.S. Kidd* docked at the river front, aiming their cannons at the Exxon Refinery. Two other Spanish Town residents, Ted and Margot Hicks, formed the Krewe of Yazoo, a precision lawn mower brigade that every year finds new ways to play on the word mow: "Mowdana," "Roach Mowtel," "Cosmownauts," and so forth. "There was an undercurrent of reaction to the suburbanization of Baton Rouge," Spitzer says, "to its straightness, to its refineries, to its militarism. All that good stuff was thrown in the soup and served up."

Notwithstanding the lewd irreverence, the parade grew exponentially. "The first year there were probably about 400 participants," Spitzer says. "The next year there were 800, and the year after that 1,500." By the late eighties most of Baton Rouge was clamoring to join the fun. The year "Louisiana's Dirty Laundry" was the theme, the owner of a chain of dry cleaning establishments lobbied to be king and appeared at the annual ball wearing plastic cleaning bags. In 1994, an estimated 100,000 Baton Rougeans, a lot of them families, thronged downtown streets to view such floats as the Krewe of Maytag and the Krewe of Whackers (heavy on Lorena Bobbit and Tonya Harding themes).[3]

The Krewe of Bamboozers has paraded in Spanish Town Mardi Gras since 1990. Margot Hicks describes them as "retired white collar types with money who are some serious party people." Perennial king, Bill Noonan, a retired educational consultant in the field of adult recreation and alcohol abuse, says they really started out as a travel club. They evolved into a social group during a sightseeing trip to Avery Island, with its lush gardens of fast growing bamboo. "Somehow or another," Noonan explains, "somebody suggested not only the bamboo but the booze that we were drinking on the chartered bus and came up with Bamboozers. We do take pride in making fun of state government."[4]

Lampooning politicians is an old Louisiana tradition. If the satire has recently become more biting, it is because Lent has descended on the state budget.

In the Bayou State enjoyment and politics are so closely intertwined, Louisianians seldom think twice about incorporating civic monuments into their cultural rituals. Longite populism has leveled the wall separating the personal and the political. Just as Louisianians observe first name familiarity with elected officials, so they transgress traditional boundaries regarding public buildings.

Their sense of ownership in government is strong, and they see nothing wrong with the people appropriating its symbols for their own pleasure. During the 1990 Yuletide, for example, state authorities festooned Huey's capitol and its manicured park with more than a million Christmas lights. Although the display flaunted Puritan notions of civic decorum, it was flamboyantly democratic.

The Christmas decorations were on loan from Al Copeland, founder of Popeye's Fried Chicken. His suburban neighbors had sued him after his front yard decorations, which included gigantic reindeer, began attracting Superdome size crowds. In 1985, the state supreme court ordered Copeland to pull the plug. After the U.S. Supreme Court denied his appeal, he lobbied the Louisiana Legislature to exempt his yard display from public nuisance laws, and he came within two votes of victory.[5] When the State Agricultural Commissioner's office later suggested he move his Christmas decorations to the capitol, to honor Louisiana troops participating in Operation Desert Shield, Copeland responded warmly.[6]

Inmates from Angola penitentiary were brought in to hang the electronic holly. Near Huey's statue, they wrapped a huge "patriotic tree" with gold lights and yellow ribbons. More than 15,000 spectators, including Governor Buddy Roemer, showed up for the switch-flipping ceremony. The surreal display was "like a spirit," the Governor said. "These lights say something. I'm proud to be here."[7]

Some cultural rituals are unique to Louisiana, like igniting wooden pyramids along the Mississippi levee on Christmas Eve to light Santa's way down river. Today hundreds of blazes illuminate the levee between Baton Rouge and New Orleans. Ronald St. Pierre pioneered the construction of non-traditional bonfire designs, such as riverboats and trucks. Because levee authorities were dilatory in issuing bonfire licenses for the 1993 Christmas season, St. Pierre was left with too little time to build a complicated design.[8] Conceived to dominate the flat landscape, Huey's monument jumped out at him on his drive home from Baton Rouge in late November. "I just happened to look at the state capitol and said to myself, 'Well, that's going to be a quick one right here.' The next day is when I started it."

St. Pierre invited the governor to attend the bonfire, but Edwards never showed up. Tourists from 45 states and 23 countries were on hand, though. "A lot of guys pulled over on the side of the road because it was so high and all," St. Pierre says of his log capitol. Old-timers were impressed by how evenly the structure burned. "It fell perfect. It had no logs that rolled out on the levee or nothing."[9]

Louisiana is a land of incongruities. Rural pilgrims to Huey's bullet-pocked shrine jostle good-naturedly with power brokers. School children brush past lobbyists huddling with lawmakers. Meanwhile, back at the old place, yuppie suburbanites picnic beside Dakin's cast-iron fence while working-class blacks boogie on the terrace. "Louisiana culture looks conservative on the surface," says folklorist Spitzer, "but once you get into it, you discover people have a lot of personal freedom, and flamboyant statements of all types are just allowed to happen."

Common ground in Louisiana has always been politics and pleasure, and her capitols, which never escaped New Orleans' epicurean orbit, have furnished the settings. That cultural role has been the saving grace of Huey's personalized monument to social realism. No one has ever said, as a Swedish poet did of Warsaw's Soviet-built Palace of Culture, that the skyscraper capitol "radiates coldness and represents emptiness."[10] The building has been absorbed into the life of the people.

A couple celebrating Fourth of July
walks along the Mississippi levee in
Baton Rouge.

Fourth of July festivities near the
Old State Capitol

Steps leading to the Capitol's front
entrance bear the names of the
50 states and their dates of
admission to the Union.

The observation platform at the top of the State Capitol affords a panoramic view of the Mississippi River and downtown Baton Rouge.

Pentagon Barracks at sundown

Lee Lawrie's sculptures of sugar and cotton workers form the base of the architrave that wraps around the Capitol's front portal.

In 1990, fried chicken magnate Al
Copelin joined forces with Agriculture
Commissioner Bob Odom to transform
the Capitol and grounds into a
Christmas landscape.

Santa Claus and his reindeer land on the Louisiana Senate as "The Pioneers" sculpture is washed in Christmas lights.

Christmas lights illuminate the Huey
Long statue in front of the Capitol.

Renowned bonfire builder Ronald St. Pierre constructed a replica of the State Capitol from cut logs. Traditionally, on Christmas Eve, hundreds of bonfire structures burn along the Mississippi levee between Baton Rouge and New Orleans.

Thousands of students visit the
Louisiana State House each year.

Baton Rouge Blues Festival

Float riders don pink flamingos as
head pieces for the Spanish Town
Mardi Gras parade.

As king of Spanish Town Mardi Gras parade in 1983, auto dealer Price LeBlanc walks among his subjects.

Mardi Gras revelers poke fun at gambling legislation.

While the official 1994 parade theme was "neatness counts," popular expression focused on newsmaker Lorena Bobbit, allowing the Krewe of Snafu to comment on both Louisiana politics and the Capitol's phallic shape.

The Magnolia Grand Brass Band
line up next to float riders
donning KKK costumes before the
Spanish Town Mardi Gras parade
begins. The 1992 theme, following
the Edwards/Duke gubernatorial
election, was "Beneath the Sheets."

Mardi Gras celebrants wear the images of Reverend Jimmy Swaggart, David Duke, and Governor Edwin Edwards as they prepare to march in the 1992 Spanish Town Mardi Gras parade.

The Krewe of Yazoo precision lawn mower drill team practices a mower maneuver in the 1992 Spanish Town Mardi Gras parade. Each year the organization selects a theme that contains the word or concept "mow." In this photo they paraded as the "Roach Mow-tels". In previous years, they mowed their way through the parade route as "Carmen Mow-randas" or icons from "Grace-lawn."

Goose stepping past the Old State
Capitol in 1993, members of the
Krewe of Yazoo don Soviet space suits
to pay tribute to "Cos-mow-nauts."

The State Capitol reflects the last light of day.

SPECIAL THANKS

This book would not have been possible without help from the following people.

Kathy Ashworth

Rudy Baudoin

Hal Beridon

Jason Berry

Tom Bertuccini

Armand Brinkhaus

Roger Busbice

Joan Caldwell

Richard Campbell

Joyce Cheney

Marie Constantin

Bob Courtney

David Culbert

Terry De Ben

Silvia Duke

Randy Haynie

Lance Hill

Pat and Jean Hurley

Sailor Jackson

Don Kurtz

Patrick and Elizabeth Little

W. Ross and Marcie Little

Joe Logsdon

Eean McNaughton

John Maginnis

Pat Maney

Judith Meriwether

Sid Moreland

Jim and Lily Morrow

James Olivier

Diana Powell

Mary Louise Prudhomme

Larry Sides

Dick Thevenot

Joe Tregle

Kevin Williams

John Wright

Troy Yarborough

ENDNOTES

CAPITOL WANDERINGS

[1] Henry C. Castellanos, *New Orleans As It Was*, foreword by Charles L. Dufour (Gretna, LA: Pelican Publishing Co., 1990 [1895], 20-26; John Smith Kendall, *History of New Orleans*, I (Chicago and New York: The Lewis Publishing Company, 1922), 121 and 132.

[2] *Debates of the Convention of 1845*, 383.

[3] Ibid., 396.

[4] Ibid., 395.

[5] Arthur Scully, Jr., *James Dakin, Architect: His Career in New York and the South* (Baton Rouge: LSU Press, 1973), 132-3.

[6] New Orleans *Daily Picayune*, February 18, 1846, p. 2 (for the quotation); March 3, 1846, p. 2; March 5, 1846, p. 2. Also *Journal of the House of Representatives of the State of Louisiana. 1846* (New Orleans, 1846),38-9, 42-3; *Journal of the Senate of Representatives of the State of Louisiana. 1846* (New Orleans, 1846), 23-5, 47-9. *Louisiana Session Laws, 1845-6*, 4.

[7] New Orleans *Daily Picayune*, July 1 & 2, 1879.

LOUISIANA GOTHIC

[1] Henry-Russell Hitchcock and William Seale, *Temples of Democracy: The State Capitols of the USA* (New York and London: Harcourt Brace Jovanovich, 1976), 76.

[2] Jesse Poesch, *The Art of the Old South* (New York: Alfred A. Knopf, 1983), 215; Arthur Scully, Jr., *James Dakin, Architect: His Career in New York and the South* (Baton Rouge: LSU Press, 1973), 126-7; Talbot Hamlin, *Greek Revival Architecture* (London and New York: Oxford University Press, 1944), 230.

[3] The standard biography is Scully, *James Dakin*, especially pp. 39-67, 85-161.

[4] Eean McNaughton, "More on the Old State Capitol," [New Orleans] *Preservation in Print* (August, 1994), 19.

[5] Calder Loth and Julius T. Sadler, Jr., *The Only Proper Style: Gothic Architecture in America* (Boston: New York Graphic Society, 1975), 42-3; Roland G. Osterweis, *Romanticism and Nationalism in the Old South* (New Haven: Yale University Press, 1949), 162-4; Roger P. McCutcheon, "Books and Book Sellers in New Orleans, 1730-1830," *Louisiana Historical Quarterly*, 20 (July 1937), 617; Harold F. Bogner, "Sir Walter Scott in New Orleans, 1818-1832," in *ibid.*, 21 (April, 1938), 420-517, the quotation is on page 441.

[6] Scully, *James Dakin*, 150-1

[7] Louisiana *Courier*, April 14, 1847, p 2.

[8] The history of the capitol's construction is ably told in Scully, *James Dakin*, 128-46.

[9] Ibid., 137 and 185. See also *Old State Capitol: Historic Structures Report* (New Orleans: McNaughton & Associates, May 14, 1984 [privately printed]).

[10] New Orleans, *Daily Delta*, Feb. 13, 1852, p. 1; New Orleans, *Daily Crescent*, Feb. 12, 1852, p. 2.

[11] Quoted in Scully, *Dakin*, 188.

[12] Ibid., 152-3.

[13] "William Freret," in *A Dictionary of Louisiana Biography*, ed. by Glenn R. Conrad, vol. I (Lafayette, LA: USL Press, 1988), 325.

[14] *American Architect and Building News* 89 (June 16, 1906), p. 197.

[15] Twain, *Life on the Mississippi*, with an afterword by Leonard Kriegel (New York: The New American Library, 1961), 237-8.

[16] *Old State Capitol: Historic Structures Report*, 44-6. McNaughton, "More on the Old State Capitol," 16.

[17] "Architecture in America," in *Architectural Forum* (April, 1956); "Louisiana Fantasy," *Architectural Review* (May, 1967), 385.

[18] *Old State Capitol: Historic Structures Report*, 11.

[19] Interview with Eean McNaughton, September 9, 1994.

[20] Interview with Kevin Harris, September 2, 1994.

[21] Interview with Bob Courtney, September 2, 1994.

[22] McNaughton, "More on the Old State Capitol," 16-7.

[23] Interview with Bill Allerton, October 11, 1994.

[24] Interview with James Sefcik, September 3, 1994. "Old State Capitol Suffers From the Economic Slump," New Orleans *Times-Picayune*, August 7, 1988; James F. Sefcik, "Board is Trying to Do Justice to an Outstanding Facility," Baton Rouge *Sunday Advocate*, April 29, 1990.

[25] Interview with Brian Kendrick, October 9, 1994.

[26] Interview with Mike Baer, October 7, 1994.

[27] T. Harry Williams, *Huey Long* (New York: Alfred A. Knopf, 1969), 427.

MONUMENTS AND MEMORY

[1] Interview with Solis Seiferth, 1972 Program of the Louisiana Heritage Committee, Louisiana Architects Association; Jack Wardlaw, "The Capitol is 50 Years Old," New Orleans *Times-Picayune*, April 4, 1982.

[2] Allan P. Sindler, *Huey Long's Louisiana: State Politics, 1920-1952* (Baltimore and London, The Johns Hopkins Press, 1956), 102-8; Alan Brinkley, *Voices of Protest: Huey Long, Father Coughlin, and the Great Depression* (New York: Alfred A. Knopf, 1983), passim.

[3] Alexdei Tarkhanov and Sergei Kavtardadze, *Architecture of the Stalin Era* (New York: Rizzoli International Publications, 1992), 9-10; Barbara Miller Lane, *Architecture and Politics in Germany, 1918-1945* (Cambridge: Harvard University Press, 1968).

[4] T. Harry Williams, *Huey Long* (New York: Alfred A. Knopf, 1969), 427-8, 447-85; *Every Man a King: The Autobiography of Huey P. Long*, with an intro. by T. Harry Williams (Chicago: Quadrangle Books, 1964), 236-9; Vincent F. Kubly, *The Louisiana Capitol: Its Art and Architecture* (Gretna, LA: Pelican Publishing Company, 1977), 23.

[5] Williams, *Huey Long*, 428.

[6] Henry-Russell Hitchcock and William Seale, *Temples of Democracy: The State Capitols of the USA* (New York and London: Harcourt Brace Jovanovich, 1976), 272-4; "The South's New Skyscraper Capitol," *The Architectural Forum* (December, 1932), 520-34.

[7] Kubly, *The Louisiana Capitol*, 25-6; Jonathan Fricker, "Louisiana Architecture: The Art Deco Style," [New Orleans] *Preservation in Print* (June, 1994), 6-8; Roger Green, "Ornate Capitol is a Tower of Style," New Orleans *Times-Picayune*, August 1, 1981.

[8] Weiss, Dreyfous & Seiferth to Huey Long, February 17, 1930, "Huey Long folder," State Capitol Boxes, Southeastern Architectural Archives, Howard-Tilton Library, Tulane University.

[9] Hitchcock and Seale, *Temples of Democracy*, 229-30, 272-8.

[10] "Capitol Built By New Orleans Men," New Orleans *Item-Tribune* (Capitol Edition), May 15, 1932, p. 10.

[11] Weiss to Julius Dreyfous and Solis Seiferth, December 13, 1931, Box 1, folder 9, State Capitol Boxes.

[12] W. G. Distler to Leon Weiss, April 29, 1931; Weiss to Distler, May 4, 1931, in Box 9, "Progress Schedule file," State Capitol Boxes.

[13] Hamlin Garland, "The Art of Lorado Taft," in Box 37, Professional Correspondence, Angela Gregory Papers, Southeastern Architectural Archives, Howard-Tilton Library, Tulane University. Also, Walter Raymond Agar, *The New Architectural Sculpture* (New York: Oxford University Press, 1935), 36-8.

[14] Leon C. Weiss to Lorado Taft, January 28, 1932; Taft to Weiss, January 30, 1932; in Box 1, "Lorado Taft folder." Ulric Ellerhusen to Weiss, May 21, 1931, Box 1, "Ulric Ellerhusen folder," State Capitol Boxes.

[15] Weiss to Ulric Ellerhusen, March 11, 1932, Box 1, "Ellerhusen folder," State Capitol Boxes.

[16] The controversies appear in the lengthy correspondence between Lawrie in Weiss, in Box 1, "Lee Lawrie folder," State Capitol Boxes. For the quotations see Weiss to Lawrie, May 19, 1931, January 20 and 27, 1932; and Lawrie to Weiss, January 23, 1932.

[17] For representative samples see Weiss to Piccirilli Brothers, June 5 and October 5, 1931, Box 1, folder 6; Weiss to Ulric Ellerhusen, May 21 and June 3, 1931, Box 1, "Ellerhusen folder," State Capitol Boxes.

[18] Weiss to Piccirilli brothers, March 14, 1931, Box 1, folder 6; Ellerhusen to Weiss, March 4, 1931, Box 1, "Ellerhusen folder," State Capitol Boxes.

[19] Ellerhusen to Weiss, August 28, 1931; Weiss to Ellerhusen, August 29, 1931, Box 1, "Ellerhusen folder," State Capitol Boxes.

[20] Henry P. Dart to Leon C. Weiss, March 23, 1931, Box 2, folder 12 "Correspondence," State Capitol Boxes.

[21] Solis Seiferth to Dart, May 27, 1931, Box 2, folder 12 "Correspondence," State Capitol Boxes.

[22] Weiss to Taft, February 1 and 10, 1932; Taft to Weiss, February 14, 1932, Box 1, "Lorado Taft folder," State Capitol Boxes.

[23] Williams, *Huey Long*, 319-21; 436-7. Weiss to Weiss, Dreyfous & Seiferth, December 11, 1931; Ellerhusen to Jerome Beatty (of *American Magazine*), September 27, 1932, both in Box 1, "Ellerhusen folder," State Capitol Boxes.

[24] Williams, *Huey Long*, 563-5; *Congressional Record*, 72 Cong., 1 Sess., pp. 10394-5.

[25] "Missing Steel Supports Endanger Huey's Capitol," New Orleans *Times-Picayune*, August 22, 1993, B8.

[26] Hitchcock and Seale, *Temples of Democracy*, 284 [for the quotation]; Kubly, *The Louisiana Capitol*, 26-9; Agard, *The New Architectural Sculpture*, 37-8.

[27] William Ivy Hair, *The Kingfish and His Realm: The Life and Times of Huey P. Long* (Baton Rouge: LSU Press, 1991), 32-4.

[28] Harnett T. Kane, *Louisiana Hayride: The American Rehearsal for Dictatorship, 1928-1940*, with an introduction by Sam H. Jones (Gretna, LA: Pelican Publishing Company, 1971 [1941]), 352.

[29] Interview with Leta Marks, October 16, 1994.

[30] *Louisiana: A Guide to the State*, compiled by the WPA (New York: Hastings House Publishers, 1941), 258-9.

[31] Sindler, *Huey Long's Louisiana*, passim.

[32] John Maginnis, *The Last Hayride* (Baton Rouge: Gris Gris Press, 1984), 6-9.

[33] John Maginnis, "Going in Style," *Louisiana Political Review* (Summer, 1994), 4.

[34] Andrei Codrescu, *A Craving for Swan* (Columbus, Ohio: Ohio State University Press, 1986), 165-6.

EVERY MAN A KING

[1] John Maginnis, *The Last Hayride* (Baton Rouge: Gris Gris Press, 1984), 333-42.

[2] Interview with Nick Spitzer, October 28, 1994.

[3] Baton Rouge *Advocate*, March 1, 1992, B1.

[4] Interview with Margot Hicks, October 23, 1994; interview with Bill Noonan, October 25, 1994.

[5] The controversy is recounted in several James Gill columns: "Burning Questions on Yule Lights," December 13, 1985; "Copeland Lights and Lawmakers," May 9, 1986; "The Case of the Meddling Judge," June 13, 1986; "The Senate Decides: All Quiet on the Copeland Lawn," June 20, 1986, all in the editorial section of the New Orleans *Times-Picayune*.

[6] Interview with Bud Corson, October 24, 1994.

[7] Risa Roberts, "Christmas Lights Help Warm Up Cold, Restless Crowd at Capitol," Baton Rouge *Morning Advocate*, November 30, 1990; Christi Daugherty, "Huge Crowds Expected for Capitol Lights," Baton Rouge *State Times*, November 28, 1990, A1.

[8] Vicki Hyman, "Two Parishes Team Up for Bonfire," New Orleans *Times-Picayune*, October 27, 1994, B2.

[9] Interviews with Ronald St. Pierre, October 27, 1993, and Mayor Guy Poché, October 25, 1994.

[10] Anders Amam, *Architecture and Ideology in Eastern Europe during the Stalin Era: An Aspect of Cold War History* (Cambridge: MIT Press, 1992), 131.